POPULAR MOVIE HITS PIANO LIBRARY

Arranged by GAIL LEW and CHRIS LOBDELL

CONTENTS

TITLE	PAGE

Visit alfred.com/downloads to purchase MIDI files and
full-length audio recordings from this book

W0010815

Editor: **Gail Lew**
Production Coordinator: **Karl Bork**
MIDI and CD Background Orchestrations: **Chris Lobdell**
Art Design: **Ernesto Ebanks**
Book Art Layout: **Michael Ramsay**

From the Motion Pictures "STAR WARS" and "THE EMPIRE STRIKES BACK"
A Lucasfilm Ltd. Production-A Twentieth Century Fox Release

Star Wars
(Main Title)

Music by **JOHN WILLIAMS**
Arranged by GAIL LEW
and CHRIS LOBDELL

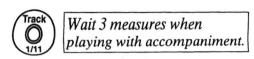

Wait 3 measures when
playing with accompaniment.

Majestic march tempo

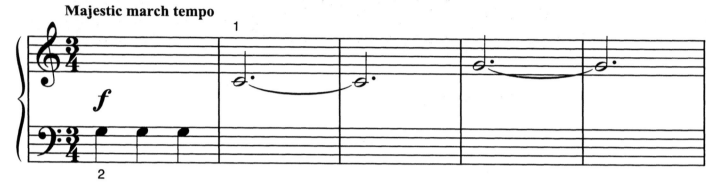

Accompaniment *(student plays one octave higher)*

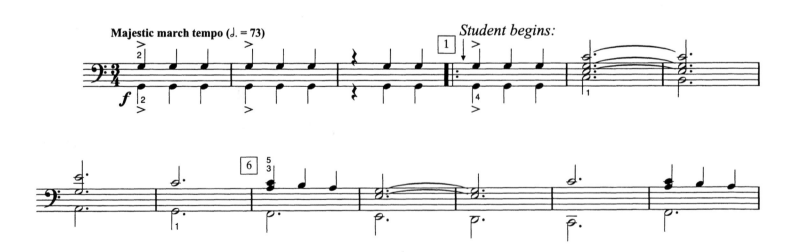

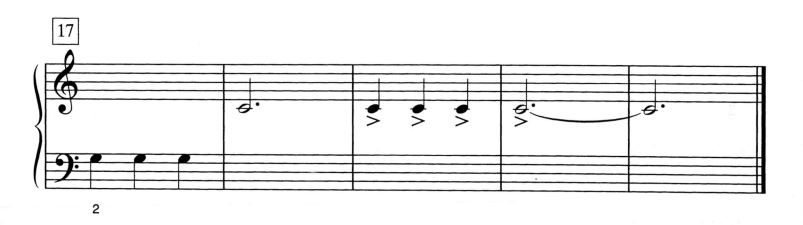

From the Warner Bros. Motion Picture "SUPERMAN"

Theme from "Superman"

Music by **JOHN WILLIAMS**
*Arranged by GAIL LEW
and CHRIS LOBDELL*

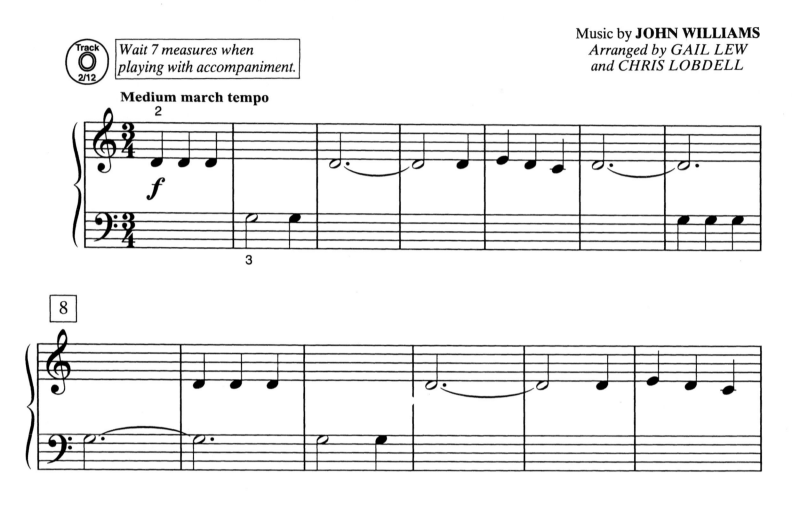

Accompaniment *(student plays one octave higher)*

ELM05005

From the MGM Motion Picture "THE WIZARD OF OZ"

Over the Rainbow

Words by E.Y. HARBURG

Music by HAROLD ARLEN
*Arranged by GAIL LEW
and CHRIS LOBDELL*

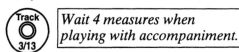

Wait 4 measures when
playing with accompaniment.

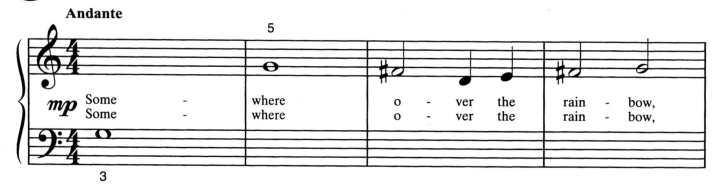

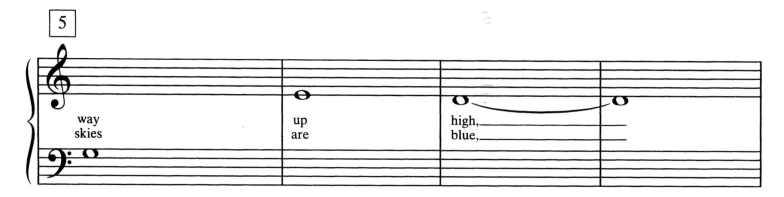

Accompaniment *(student plays one octave higher)*

7

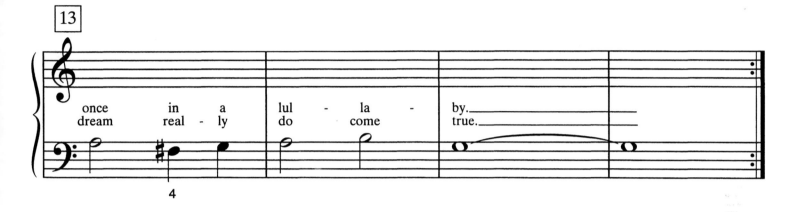

ELM05005

From the Motion Picture "THE LION KING"

The Lion Sleeps Tonight

New Lyrics and Revised Music by
GEORGE DAVID WEISS, HUGO PERETTI
and LUIGI CREATORE
Arranged by GAIL LEW
and CHRIS LOBDELL

Track 4/14

Wait 4 measures when playing with accompaniment.

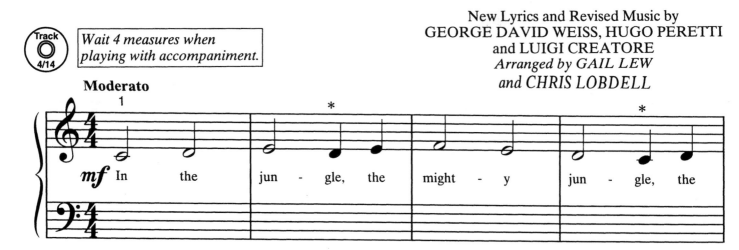

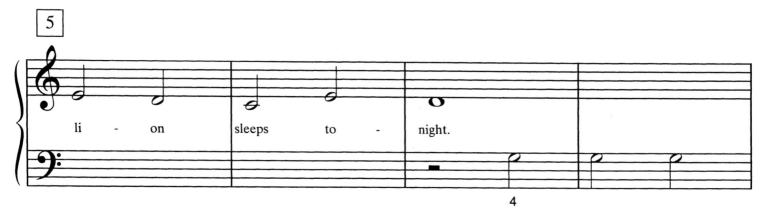

*Dotted rhythm (♩. ♪) may be taught by rote at the discretion of the teacher.

Accompaniment *(student plays one octave higher)*

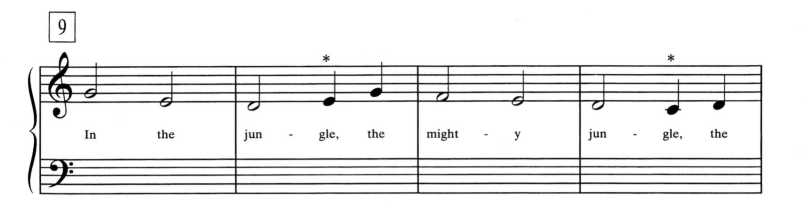

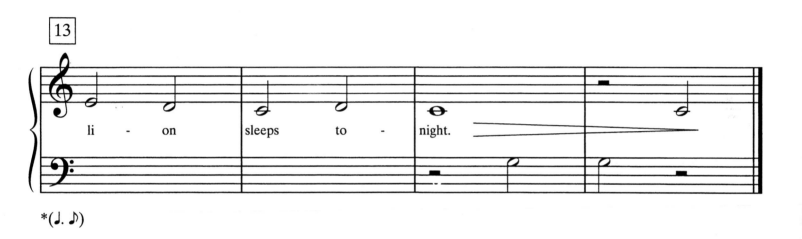

*(♩. ♪)

From the MGM Motion Picture "DIE ANOTHER DAY"

James Bond Theme

Music by MONTY NORMAN
*Arranged by GAIL LEW
and CHRIS LOBDELL*

ELM05005

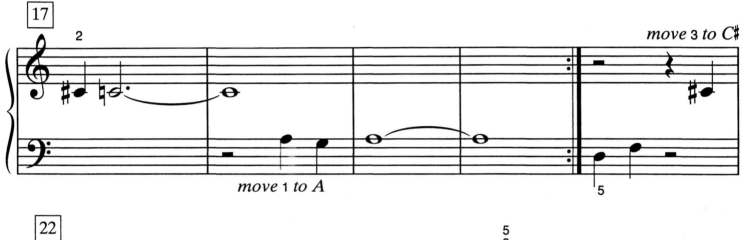

*Right-hand chord (B-C#-E) is optional and may be introduced at the discretion of the teacher.

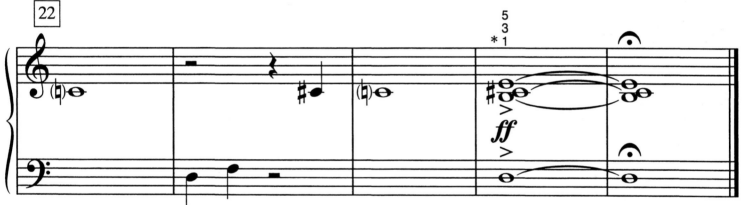

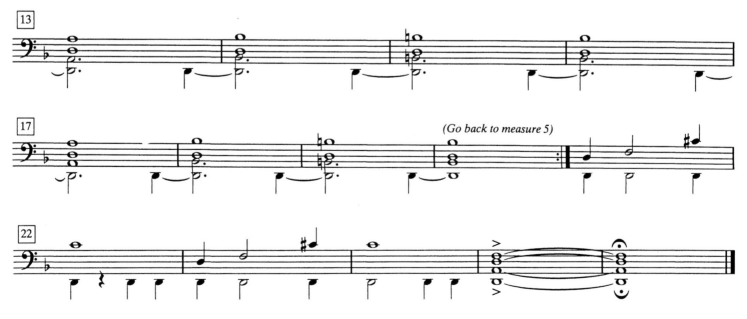

Scooby-Doo, Where Are You?

Words and Music by
DAVID MOOK and BEN RALEIGH
Arranged by GAIL LEW
and CHRIS LOBDELL

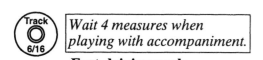

Wait 4 measures when playing with accompaniment.

Fast driving rock

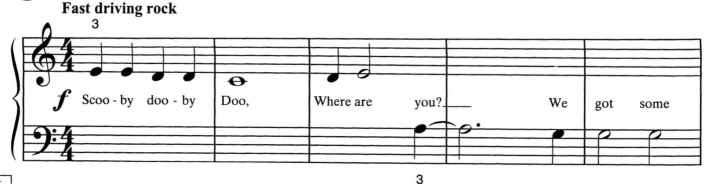

Scoo - by doo - by Doo, Where are you?___ We got some

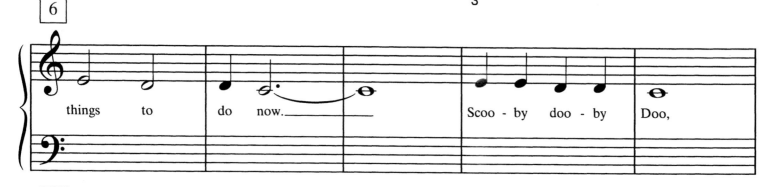

things to do now.___ Scoo - by doo - by Doo,

Where are you?___ We need some help from you now.___

Accompaniment *(student plays one octave higher)*

Fast driving rock (♩ = 116)

Student begins:

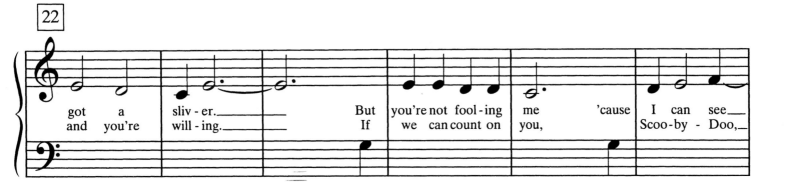

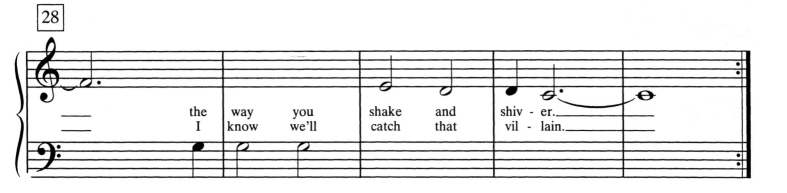

Theme Song from the Mirisch-G&E Production, "THE PINK PANTHER," a United Artist's Release

The Pink Panther

Music by
HENRY MANCINI
Arranged by GAIL LEW
and CHRIS LOBDELL

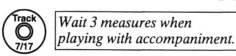

Wait 3 measures when
playing with accompaniment.

Mysterioso

move 4 to G♯

*Dotted rhythm (♪ ♩.) may be taught by rote at the discretion of the teacher.

**Long-short rhythm (♩. ♪) may be taught by rote.

Accompaniment *(student plays one octave higher)*

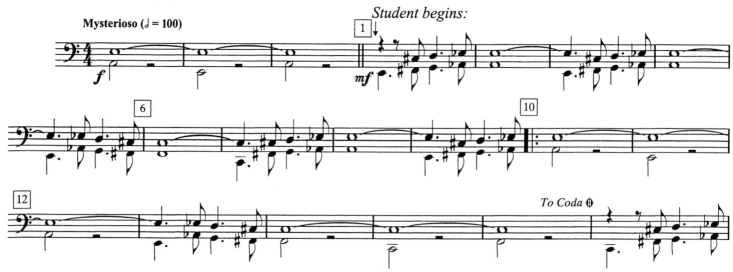

(Go back to measure 10)

(A♭ and G♯ are the same note on the keyboard.)

Coda

move 3 to G♯

*(♪ ♩.)

**Long-short rhythm (♩. ♪) may be taught by rote.

(Go back to measure 10)

Coda

ELM05005

From "HARRY POTTER AND THE CHAMBER OF SECRETS"

Fawkes the Phoenix

Music by
JOHN WILLIAMS
Arranged by GAIL LEW
and CHRIS LOBDELL

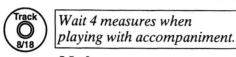

Wait 4 measures when
playing with accompaniment.

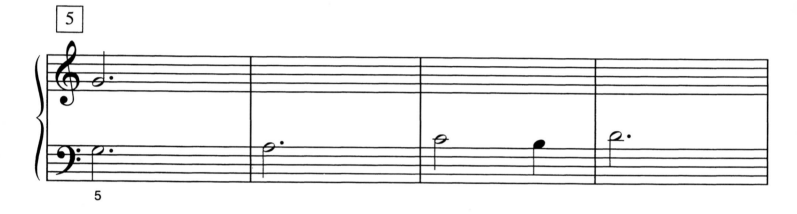

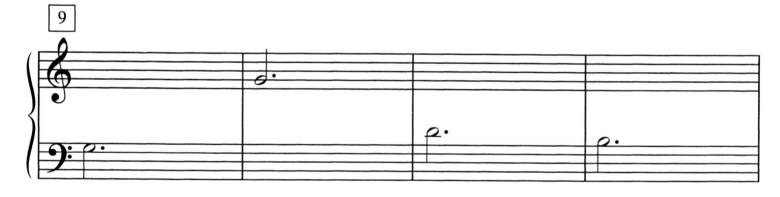

Accompaniment *(student plays one octave higher)*

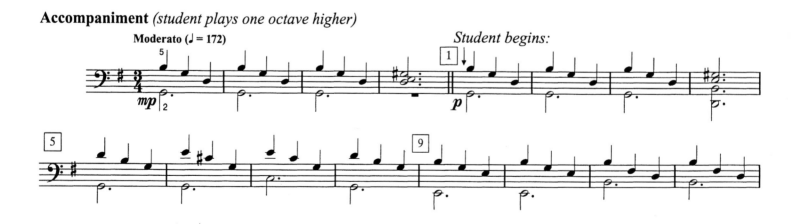

ELM05005

From "HARRY POTTER AND THE PRISONER OF AZKABAN"

A Window to the Past

Music by
JOHN WILLIAMS
Arranged by GAIL LEW
and CHRIS LOBDELL

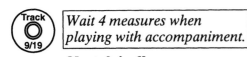

Wait 4 measures when
playing with accompaniment.

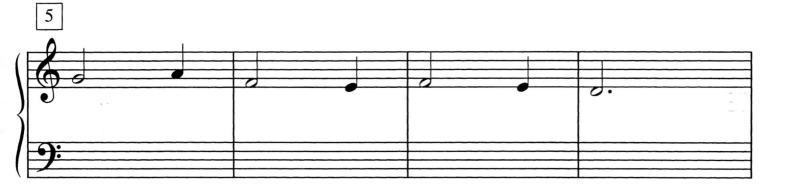

*Dotted rhythm (♩. ♪) may be taught by rote at the discretion of the teacher.

Accompaniment *(student plays one octave higher)*

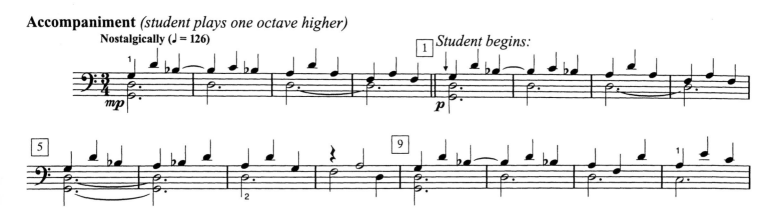

ELM05005

move 5 to D

move 1 to B

Nobly

mp

(♩. ♪)

Nobly

*(♩. ♪)

From Warner Bros. Pictures' HARRY POTTER AND THE SORCERER'S STONE

Hedwig's Theme

Music by
JOHN WILLIAMS
Arranged by GAIL LEW
and CHRIS LOBDELL

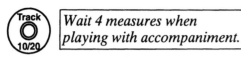

Wait 4 measures when
playing with accompaniment.

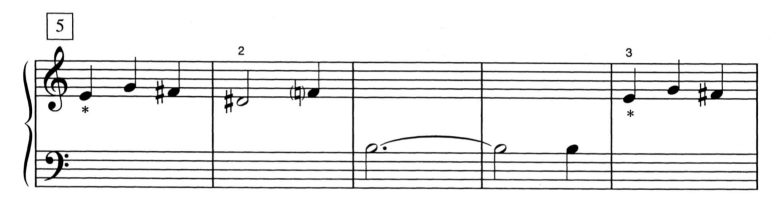

*Dotted rhythm (♩. ♪) may be taught by rote at the discretion of the teacher.

Accompaniment *(student plays one octave higher)*

*(♩. ♪)